Wisdom For People of All Faiths

10 WAYS TO CONNECT WITH GOD

By Rabbi Evan Moffic

Published by Washington Avenue Press
1301 Clavey Ave, Highland Park, IL 60035

First printing, March 2013

Editing, cover design, print layout and eBook Conversion
by YourDigitalBook.com

Dedication

This book is dedicated to my parents—Lynn and Steve Moffic. Your influence, love and wisdom permeate every page of this book. Thank you for teaching by example, and for giving every ounce of your being to loving and nurturing your family. You exemplified the Jewish ideal, summarized by our favorite teacher Jonathan Sacks: "Judaism places such emphasis on *shalom bayit*, peace in the home, because it's in the home that we are tested, there that we learn the love that is respect, consideration, gentleness, the capacity to listen as well as speak, sensitivity, graciousness and the willingness to make sacrifices for one another. It's there that we *learn chessed,* the love that is also kindness; and it's this that brings the *Shekhinah*, the Presence of God, into the home."

Table of Contents

Acknowledgements

This book comes out of my experience as a rabbi in the field. Pieces of it have appeared in sermons and articles. All of it comes from having been given the greatest gift I can imagine: the chance to work and serve as a rabbi. I thank God every day to have found a career I love, and to work with people—from my synagogue members to the lay leadership to other Jewish professionals in Chicago and around the world—who teach and inspire me every day.

In particular, the members of leadership of Congregation Solel in Highland Park, Illinois, have supported me and nurtured my love of writing, teaching and preaching. It is a rabbi's dream of a congregation, filled with bright, committed folks interesting in learning about Judaism and working in the community. I am also grateful to the members and leadership of Chicago Sinai Congregation, who hired me as an intern while I was still in rabbinical school and with whom I continue to enjoy deep and meaningful friendships.

All of this writing took time away from my family. To my wife Ari: your love makes everything possible. To our children Hannah and Tamir: you are our greatest teachers of wisdom and the depth and power of love. My amazing sister Stacia and her family—Bill, Noah, and Mira—have tolerated my inconsistent appearances at family gatherings with love and humor. Ellen and Stan are the greatest in-laws a husband could hope for—kind, dedicated, and loving in every way.

Introduction

Today we have so much information but so little wisdom. If we are to thrive and find happiness as individuals and as a community, we need more. What better place to begin than in the teachings of the world's oldest religion? That religion is Judaism, and it is the one to which I have devoted my life and my learning.

In this book, I dig deep into the Jewish wisdom tradition to highlight insights and practices we can use today. How can we live with fewer regrets? How can we find greater satisfaction and success as parents, siblings, children and friends? How can we find meaning and insight amidst endless distraction and information overload?

Whatever our faith, we need help answering these questions. There is deep wisdom in the Old Testament. That wisdom was given further expression in later commentaries and writings from Jewish sages throughout history. It is accessible, inviting and life-changing. It proclaims hope amidst despair and the personal relationship between God and every human being.

Indeed, the wisdom we will discover in Jewish tradition works for people of all faiths. In my regular column for the world's largest multi-faith website – Beliefnet.com – and in the counseling and teaching I've done in synagogues, churches and multi-faith institutions around the country, I've seen lives transformed, faith rediscovered, families renewed.

This book captures these lessons and experiences. Each chapter focuses on a different theme in which a connection with God can give us hope and greater possibilities for success. They include ways to pray with greater understanding, forgive even when it hurts and transform our anger into spiritual strength. In addressing this issues, I draw from the Jewish wisdom I have studied as well as from my professional experience "in the trenches" as the spiritual leader of a large congregation. My hope and prayer is that the stories and insights you find here will fill your lives with greater inspiration, fewer regrets and enduring happiness.

SECTION I: PRACTICES

Chapter 1: How Prayer Lifts the Ordinary into the Extraordinary

"Prayer means that, in some unique way, we believe we're invited into a relationship with someone who hears us when we speak in silence." Anne Lamott

We often think of prayer as asking for things. As Chicago comic Emo Philips once joked, "When I was a kid I used to pray every night for a new bicycle. Then I realized that the Lord doesn't work that way so I stole one and asked Him to forgive me."

While humorous, this view of prayer belittles it. In Judaism, prayer is not primarily about asking God for things. *It is about remembering what things in life are most important.* Just as mission statements highlight the purpose and values of an organization, our prayers proclaim the values by which we strive to live.

One of the foremost of these values is gratitude. Prayer helps us rejoice in what we have, rather than focus incessantly on what we do not yet have. Toward this end, *in Judaism, prayer is directed not so much at God as it is at ourselves.* When we pray, we look at our lives from an elevated perspective, from what the philosopher Spinoza called the point of view of eternity. To use a familiar metaphor, prayer lifts us out of the trees so we can look at the forest.

Prayer Gives Us A New Language

Prayer also helps us express feelings that everyday words cannot. When I officiate at a funeral, I always notice the mourners during the recitation of the 23rd Psalm. As we say the words, "Yea, though I walk through the valley of the shadow of death, I will fear no evil, for thou art with me," faces turn downward. Tears often begin to flow. The words of prayer evoke emotions that ordinary language cannot.

At its best, prayer gives us access to a range of emotions we often overlook. Prayer connects us with the entire spiritual, emotional and intellectual library of our faith. When we pray with resolve, feeling the words shaping us, we are dancing. We are moving to the words of our sages. Do we really need to dance to these words? Can they really make difference in our lives?

Well, as one rabbi put it, "Neither the computer nor the cellular phone has changed the fact of mortality or the want of wisdom." *In an age of high technology, we need to be reminded of what truly matters. Prayer is that reminder.* It reminds us that our lives are measured by holiness. Prayer gives us a glimpse of something higher, and helps us become what we are capable of being.

Proof for the Power of Prayer

Something magical happens in our home on Friday night. The bustle of the week stops. The noise of dinnertime fades away. The iPad powers down (at least for a while).

What changes everything is the moment we put our hands on our children and say a blessing over them. The blessing is short, personal and changes every week. Its impact, however, is almost always the same: a smile, a hug and a relaxed look of joy.

It's not the words themselves that are magical. It is the words together with the mood and the people.

The old saying goes "A family that prays together stays together." While experience and reflection make that statement seem simplistic for me, the truth is that prayer creates a unique feeling of kinship and joy. It helps children feel connected and secure, and it reminds adults that there is more to life than constant activity. Prayer puts life in perspective.

How Prayer Works

Some might argue that the purpose of prayer is not to make us feel better, but rather, to speak to God. This view of prayer is far too limiting. In fact, the Hebrew word *li-hit-palel* means "to pray," and it falls into the category of what linguists called "reflexive verbs." That means that the direct object of the verb "to pray" is ourselves. When we pray, we are shaping ourselves.

Prayer can also help us make better decisions. Malcolm Gladwell talked about the way we make decisions in his book *Blink*. We usually make decisions about people, purchases or what to say in the blink of an eye. In other words, we do not think much about it. We act by instinct. Where do these instincts come from? How are they developed? We develop them through education. We learn them from our parents. And we can hone them with prayer.

Prayer is not always literal. In Judaism, for example, when we say, for example, that God heals the sick, we are not envisioning God as a cosmic physician. We are reminding ourselves of the sacredness of life and of the relationships that matter most. We are reminding ourselves that we are meant to live, and that our words and actions can help heal others. God heals through us.

One of the core principles of a life of faith is that life is a gift. This truth is embedded in Judaism. The Hebrew word for Judaism is *"yehadut,"* which shares its linguistic root with *"hodaot,"* the Hebrew word for "thanksgiving." In other words, Judaism means thanksgiving. Giving thanks is one of the core ways we express our faith.

Prayer is the primary way we do that. We thank God for our breath, for a functioning body, for life and for teaching us how to live. Among our most religious acts is saying "thank you."

Prayer Connects Us To God

The nineteenth century English poet, Matthew Arnold, described God as the "power greater than ourselves that makes for righteousness." By describing God as a "power," Arnold suggests that God gives direction and energy to human existence.

By seeing that power as "greater than ourselves," Arnold acknowledges that God is not limited by the natural world. God both exists in the world and transcends it. In other words, we can experience God in our lives, but we can never say precisely what God is.

I love this approach because it forces us to be humble. God cannot be captured by any one creed or set of beliefs. God is too big for that. Yet, God is not so big and mysterious as to be irrelevant. God's relevance and power are made real by our acts of righteousness.

Does God hear our prayers? Yes, but only if we hear them, too.

Chapter 2: The Bible Is For Everyone

"So long as the Jewish people never stop learning, the Jewish heart will never stop beating." Jonathan Sacks

A great rabbi once said, "When I pray, I speak to God. When I study, God speaks to me." Studying, learning and engaging with the Bible is the next step to finding God.

The Bible is not just for pastors, priests and rabbis. It is for everyone. Studying it enriches our lives. It connects us with our past, present and future. The hardest part is usually beginning. We can come up with any number of excuses to not begin. We don't have the time. We don't know enough to start. Yet, if we want to study and gain knowledge, we can find the time. And we can start wherever we are most comfortable.

How do we make our study more meaningful and exciting?

1. Use a commentary: In Jewish tradition, we never study only the biblical text itself. We study with the interpretations of the great teachers of Jewish history. Some might say this prejudices our point of view. Shouldn't we encounter the text with fresh eyes? I would argue that we benefit from the wisdom and insights of generations past. We can and will arrive at our own interpretations and conclusions. Rather than prejudice us, the insights of great teachers will spark our own ideas and lead us to a deeper encounter with the text.

2. Study with a partner: Good partners will not only hold us accountable for taking the time to study, they will also engage us in conversation and debate. They will notice things we did not. As the Book of Ecclesiastes says, "Two is better than one."

3. Set a fixed time for study: What gets scheduled is more likely to get done. If we find a consistent time for study, we can fall into a regular pattern. In Jewish tradition, the Sabbath has always been a time for study of the weekly biblical reading; I lead a regular Saturday morning study group.

4. Use a good translation: Every translation is an interpretation. When we study the Old Testament in Hebrew or the New Testament in Greek, we can better appreciate the poetry and literary beauty of the text. However, unless we went to Divinity school, we probably do not read or write in either language. Thus, a good translation is critical.

Aim for one that seeks to preserve the cadence and character of the original. One of the best Hebrew Bible translations was done by Everett Fox, who sought to preserve much of the wordplay and poetry from the original language.

5. Say a prayer before you begin: Studying the Bible is not like studying Shakespeare. It begins and ends with faith. It is part of our search for truth and wisdom. Rather than just sit down and begin reading, I prefer to say a prayer to put myself in the proper state of mind.

In Jewish tradition, the prayer reads, *"Blessed Are You, Eternal God, Sovereign of the Universe, Who Commands Us To Immerse Ourselves in Learning. Amen."*

The Bible Is Your Story

What keeps the Bible alive is not just that it is the word of God. It is the word of God that speaks to and through us. The biblical characters are not just historical figures. They are models for the struggle of living a holy life here on earth. Consider the Exodus story, which Jews recount every year during a Passover Seder. Studying it can give each of us a sense of identity and purpose. The reason is that Passover is a story of a people's self-discovery and freedom. It resonated for the founding fathers of America who initially wanted the seal of the United States to be Moses leading the Israelites across the Red Sea. It resonated for slaves who yearned for freedom and expressed that yearning with the song, "Go Down, Moses." It resonates in our hearts, where we identify with those searching for freedom. And it can resonate in our spirits, in the way we live our lives.

It can do so, I think, because the Exodus story parallels the journey that takes place inside every human being. The great twentieth century rabbi Joseph Soloveitchik wrote about this in his essay "The Inner Transformation of Passover Night." In it he pointed out, "Although a person can participate only minimally in wonders affecting the workings of nature, such as the ten plagues or the splitting of the Red Sea, a person can participate in the performance of hidden miracles within his inner personality – uplifting of the soul, repentance, cleansing of the heart, renewing of the spirit." In other words, Passover speaks to our heart.

So what inner qualities do we strive for on Passover eve? What is the theme of the biblical story? The central one is empathy, a quality necessary for happiness and meaningful relationships with others and with God. Empathy is trying to understand another person. It is feeling what they feel. It is the fulfillment of what we are supposed to do when we study the Exodus story. We are supposed to imagine that *we ourselves* went forth from Egypt. *We ourselves*, not only the slaves thousands of years ago. When we taste the bitter herbs at the Passover meal, we feel the pangs of slavery. When we dip the parsley in saltwater, we feel the tears running down our face.

Participating in the Passover meal is not like attending a history lecture; it is entering a time machine.

This empathy awakens a new sensitivity within us. When we experience slavery, we feel more keenly the cruelties of those enslaved today. That means not only physical enslavement. *Political oppression is a form of enslavement. Addiction is a form of enslavement. An abusive relationship is a form of enslavement.* Each of us may be enslaved in other ways: to our work, to our possessions, to old habits that hurt us. When we experience the drama of slavery, we emerge more committed to addressing it in its various forms in the world around us. Indeed, the outer transformation as told in the Bible begets an inner transformation that in turn, generates new outer transformations. It is a cycle that has continued for thousands of years.

Studying The Bible Gives Us Hope

Without hope, the Israelites would never have journeyed from slavery to freedom. Indeed, looked at critically, their faith in God and Moses demonstrated in the Exodus story seems absurd!

Here they were, slaves for 400 years. Along comes a man – with a lisp – who is going to speak on their behalf before Pharaoh. He had grown up in Pharaoh's palace, but was, of late, a shepherd in the wilderness; he is saying that God has instructed him to lead all 1.2 million of them across the desert to freedom. Yet, they had hope.

The Bible gives it to us as well. Its words have power. They tell us who we are and where we are going. In telling this story of stories, we evoke within ourselves the ability to transform the world around us. Looking outward leads to looking inward.

Looking inward and responding to what we find is not easy or quick. But it is essential.

> "When I was young," recalled a great nineteenth century rabbi, "I wanted to change the world. I tried, but the world did not change. So I tried to change my town, but my town did not change. Then I turned to my family, but my family did not change. Then I realized: in order to change the world, first I must change myself: and I am still trying."

The Exodus story, and the entire Bible, teaches us about the human power to hope and change.

Chapter 3: The Life-Changing Power of Love

"Love is the one door that leads to heaven." Robert Kirschner

A story is told about former President Calvin Coolidge. He attended services at a church one Sunday morning. A friend asked him later what the preacher talked about. He paused for a second. "Sin," he replied. The friend then asked: "Well, anything particular about sin?" President Coolidge thought for a minute: "He's against it."

My subject is love. To summarize my arugment in one sentence, you could say, "I'm for it."

The Hebrew word for love is *ahava*. It is not mentioned in the Adam and Eve story. It doesn't come up with Noah. The first time we hear it is in the story of Abraham's near sacrifice of his son, Isaac. God calls out to Abraham and says, "Take your son, the son *whom you love*, and bring him up to me as a sacred offering."

The story of a near sacrifice of a son by his father may seem a strange place to introduce the idea of love. When I first noticed it, I wondered why and what for? By placing the first mention of love in this story, is the Bible trying to teach us a lesson about the meaning of love? Absolutely.

The Difference Between Self-Love and Love of Self

In order to appreciate what our tradition teaches, however, we need to start with a different verse. It is the Torah's most famous message about love. In Leviticus 19 we read: *v'ahavta l're-ehca kamocha*. This verse is typically translated, "...you shall love your neighbor as yourself." The meaning of this verse was explicated later by Rabbi Akiba, who said, "What is hateful to you, do not do to another."

Yet, consider an assumption underlying this verse, an assumption rarely explored. The assumption is that we love ourselves. Indeed, to fulfill the commandment to love another person as we love ourselves, we first need to love ourselves. An analogy that helps us understand this is the announcement we hear before airplanes take off. The flight attendant says: "Put on your own oxygen mask before assisting others." We need to be healthy – to be functioning – before we can care for another. If we are impaired, we cannot help someone else.

The same logic applies to love. Unless we can accept ourselves and value ourselves – love ourselves – we will not know how to love another.

Before we get too much further, an important distinction is in order. There is a tremendous difference between selfishness and self-love. Selfishness focuses inward. Self-love radiates outward. In fact, Erich Fromm, in his classic book, *The Art of Loving*, defines them as opposites. Selfish people think only of what interests and benefits themselves. They look at others solely in terms of their usefulness. They look outside for what is missing inside.

Genuine self-love, however, begins within. It accepts and appreciates who we are and what we can become. It helps us form a vision of our higher selves.

How do we love ourselves? First, we focus on the unique gifts we bring to the world. This is harder than it sounds. If I were to hold up a big white posterboard with a small black dot near the side, most of us would focus on that dot. We look at what's wrong rather than what's right.

We do the same thing to ourselves. We focus on our weaknesses rather than our strengths, our inevitable failures rather than our many gifts, what we do wrong rather than what we do right.

The Joy of Complaining

Sometimes we even derive an odd satisfaction in this approach. This truth is illustrated in a classic Jewish story I heard first from Rabbi Jonathan Sacks. It concerns a man named Finkelstein. He was a patient at Mass General Hospital, one of the finest hospitals in the world. He received care there for seven days. Then, without explanation, he checked himself out and checked into a run-down hospital on the Lower East Side of New York.

His new doctor was intrigued. He asked Finkelstein: "What was wrong with Mass General? Was it the doctors?"

"The doctors? They were geniuses," Finkelstein replied. "Wonderful. I can't complain."

"How about the nurses?"

"The nurses? Fantastic. Angels in human forms. Kind, attentive. About the nurses, I can't complain."

"Was it the food?" the doctor asked incredulously.

"The food was divine. Like a world-class restaurant. About the food, I can't complain."

The doctor looked frustrated. He asked Finkelstein: "Why did you leave one of the greatest hospitals in the world and come here?"

Finkelstein looked at him with a big smile. "Because here, here I can complain!"

When look at our lives and ourselves, we can complain. But it won't make us any happier or more loving. It will only block our vision. Our faith can enhance our vision. It reminds us that we are created in the image of God. It reminds us of our purpose as people – as husbands, wives, children, friends, grandparents, citizens. Through prayer and acts of love and kindness, we bring to the foreground what so often remains in the background. We try to remember, as Rabbi Yehuda Kirzner put it, "All of life is a challenge of not being distracted from the greatness that we are."

How Your Imperfection is Your Greatest Strength

That is not to say that we are perfect. In order to love ourselves, we have to accept ourselves. We need to see and acknowledge our imperfections. Jewish legend tells of a man named Zusya. He was not the best dresser nor the most well-spoken. A person asked him why he did not carry himself with more dignity. He replied: "When I get to Heaven, they will not say, 'Zusya, why were you not Moses?' They'll ask me, 'Zusya, why weren't you Zusya?'"

A funeral I once conducted echoed this story. The man who died had been an elementery school teacher and author of over 300 children's books. His children told me of his penchant for wearing the same red sweatshirt they had purchased for him decades ago. On it were the words "One Hot Firecracker." They spoke of his tendency to quote Sam Adams – about whom he had written seven books – as if he were an old friend.

Yet, as they laughed, they also spoke of his integrity, honesty, dedication to teaching students, friendships, and character inside and out. He knew who he was. He loved who he was. And others loved him for it.

When we love ourselves, we love ourselves for who we are, not who we pretend or are expected to be. Our genuine selves become a source of strength.

What Happens When We Experience Love?

The third step is not something we can do. It is only something we can experience. Part of what makes us able to love ourselves is feeling the love of others. During the Summer Olypmics in 2012, a video caught my eye.

It begins with a woman biking in the rain. Then we hear snippets of different languages as mothers begin to wake up their groggy children in bed. The same moms prepare meals, drive their children to the gymnasium, dance practice, the pool and the volleyball court. As the underlying piano music grows in volume, we see the children practicing their strokes, dance routines and volleyball spikes. Moms and dads watch them with baited breath, and then the video flashes to crowds erupting in cheers as the same children compete in front of massive audiences. It closes with tears streaming down the faces of proud parents and children, as they hug and smile.

The children did not automatically become great athletes. The love they received helped them become the people they are. All of us need such love. It doesn't matter if we are young or old, rich or poor, athletes or couch potatoes. When we experience love – when we give and receive it – we find God.

The Jewish sages make this quite explicit. In interpreting the verse that human beings are created *b'tselem elohim* – in the image of God – they ask the question: where did God place that image? Where is it? In our face, in our mouth, in our nose? No. God stored it in our hearts. The heart is where we find God.

Hearing the Invisible Beating Heart of God

With this truth in mind, let us return to our initial verse. Why is love used for the first time in the adekah, the story of the binding of Isaac? Because love is so powerful, the only way we can appreciate it is to face its potential loss. The akedah is the Bible's most intimate and unvarnished depiction of one human being facing the loss of another. Through it Abraham learns the meaning of love. Commenting on this, Rabbi Jonathan Sacks observed, "We can only fully appreciate the significance of something or someone when we face their loss." The potential for loss heightens the sacredness of life.

Those of us who have lost a loved one or gone through a near-death experience know this truth. Loss brings a new urgency to life. And the only response to the inevitable loss we will face is love.

But love will not take hold of us automatically. We have to open ourselves up to its presence. We have to stop every now and then and feel it, search for it, receive it. And we have to acknowledge it. Not simply by words – but by actions.

The ancient Jewish sages understood this. They said love is stronger than death. And who can deny it? I think of the case of Nico Goodrich. Nico is one year old and has a twin sister named Kiki. When their mother, Andrea, was pregnant with the girls, she went in for a routine ultrasound, but the doctors found a problem. There was a "strange halo" around Kiki's heart and a tear in the amniotic sack. They discovered that fluid was leaking from the placenta. It was only twenty weeks into the pregnancy, so doctors told Andrea to stay in the hospital until the inevitable miscarriage.

A few days later, however, a new ultrasound revealed something extraordinary. Baby Nico, the healthier of the two, had moved. She had positioned herself directly below Kiki, so low in the womb, that her body was blocking the leak from the placenta. She stayed there for ten weeks, giving her and her sister precious time to grow. They were both delivered by C-Section at 30 weeks. A few months later they went home from the hospital in perfect health.

Before she had even the spark of life, Baby Nico carried a powerful current of love. The activity of that current cannot be monitored on an EKG. Its presence cannot be detected by a stephoscope. Its meaning cannot be captured in words. But it is undeniably, invincibly there. Its power source is not some hidden generator. It is an invisible beating heart called God.

We Are Loved By An Unending Love

Judaism has often been seen as a religion of law rather than love. According to this stereotype, the Old Testament focuses on law and punishment, while the New Testament embraces love and compassion. This is quite untrue. At the heart of Judaism is a bond of love. That love begins inside each of us, and it radiates outward to each other and to God. Rabbi Rami Shapiro captures that bond in his poem, *An Unending Love*.

> "We are loved by an unending love.
> We are embraced by arms that find us
> even when we are hidden from ourselves.
> We are touched by fingers that soothe us
> even when we are too proud for soothing.
> We are counseled by voices that guide us

even when we are too embittered to hear.
We are loved by an unending love.

We are supported by hands that uplift us
even in the midst of a fall.
We are urged on by eyes that meet us
even when we are too weak for meeting.
We are loved by an unending love.

Embraced, touched, soothed, and counseled,
Ours are the arms, the fingers, the voices;
Ours are the hands, the eyes, the smiles;
We are loved by an unending love."

Chapter 4: How To Forgive Even When It Hurts

"A healthy, loving relationship is not possible without forgiveness."
Dr. Morris Mann

The following story was told by Rabbi David Whiman:

When his mother died, Mark began to go through her belongings. Knowing she was meticulously organized, he was not surprised to find a stack of daily planners. They covered the years 1948-1997.

He began to look through them and saw a clear pattern. Every day had a list. Most items on the list had lines through them, indicating they had been completed. Incomplete ones had a circle around them.

Beginning in 1955, every October 22nd the entry "Call Sylvia" was etched at the top of the page. October 22nd was Sylvia's birthday, and Mark's mom intended to call her. But every year it remained circled in red, incomplete.

His mother, and her sister-in-law Sylvia, had had some sort of falling out. No one remembered when or why.

In 1987 the item finally had a line running through it. Underneath the entry read, "Visited the cemetery. Told Sylvia I was sorry."

How Did It Get This Way?

For 32 years two relatives could not speak to one another, even though at least one of them wanted to. It was too hard, too painful. Just imagine what life would have been like had they made amends. One less hole in a heart at the time of death. One less piece of unfinished business.

How many of us walk around with a hole in our hearts? How many of us want to forgive but can't or won't? For some, even the thought of forgiveness can generate enormous pain and resistance.

There is no three- or ten-step process for forgiving. If there were, we would all know it. There are only questions we can ask ourselves.

What Did I Do?

There is a difference between being right and being effective. We may (rightly) believe we did nothing wrong in creating the rift in a relationship. We may think our brother or our sister has rewritten history, imagining we said things we never said.

But something happened. Understanding that, and trying to appreciate the situation from the other's point of view, will help immensely in giving us strength and perspective to forgive.

Here are a couple of tips for developing that perspective:

1. Remember that it's not what you say, it's what they hear. We often think of communication as driven by what we say. We communicate, and another person listens. It's more helpful to think about it in the opposite way. The agent of communication is the listener. The message is in what he or she hears.

The popular children's game "Telephone" illustrates this truth perfectly. You remember the premise of the game? It begins with several people gathering in a circle. Someone whispers a message into the ear of the person sitting next to him. That person whispers what he heard to the person sitting next to him. The process continues until it reaches the end of the circle. The last person says out loud what he heard from the person sitting next to him. It usually differs significantly and humorously from the message that began the circle. No matter what we say, we have to be mindful of what the other party hears.

2. Recognize the power of words. In Judaism God creates the universe with words. As Genesis tells us, "God said, 'Let there be light,' and there was light." The ancient Jewish sages describe the process as "God spoke, and the world came into being."

Human beings also use words to create. We carry enormous power. The old nursery rhyme, "Sticks and stones may break my bones, but words will never hurt me," could not be further from the truth. Words create emotions that can hurt us. Words can also make and break relationships. In Jewish law, the critical part of a marriage ceremony is the moment when the groom says to the bride, "By this ring, you are consecrated unto me as wife according to the laws of God and Moses." The groom's saying those words, along with the bride's acceptance of the ring, make the marriage legal according to Jewish law.

3. Use the power of non-verbal language: We communicate a great deal in what we do not say. Some studies estimate that only nine percent of communications happens through words.

Sometimes the expression on our face undermines the words we say. Others notice it, and it changes the way our words are received. This truth also reminds us to avoid difficult discussions over e-mail. I have found that it is incredibly easy for email messages to be misread. Don't use e-mail just because it is easier. It's critical to use the appropriate medium for human communication. A message we would reject via email is one we might well accept were it delivered in person.

4. Remind yourself of times you needed forgiveness:
Forgiveness is never a one-way street. We have all had times when we did something wrong and asked another to forgive us. How did the other party's response affect us? Were we relieved at their willingness to forgive? Or did we become frustrated at their lack of response?

Am I Hurting Myself?

We tend to magnify the way others see us. We assume that what consumes our attention also consumes theirs. This truth often creates misunderstanding in a relationship. It can also impede healing and reconciliation. We think we are "teaching him a lesson" when we withhold forgiveness. We think we are achieving some kind of vengeance. We think that to forgive is to condone.

Forgiving is not condoning. It is moving on. It is removing a roadblock on our path. Forgiveness is a gift we give ourselves.

Here are some questions to ask yourself to see if not forgiving is causing you unnecessary pain:

1. Do I think about this person often? If we constantly think about something that happened years ago and we cannot do anything about it, we are making ourselves miserable. Time can heal all wounds, but only if we give it permission.

2. What else am I bringing to this situation? Psychologists have long known the power of transference. We transfer images of one person to another and relate to

them in a way neither they nor we would recognize. Are we unfairly blaming someone because we are seeing them as someone else?

3. What kind of future do I envision? Am I going to live in tension with this person for the rest of my life? If not, do something now. Don't put off until tomorrow what can be done today.

Am I Asking Too Much?

We often wait for the other person to make a move. Perhaps they hurt as we do. Perhaps we are asking for more than they are capable of, even if the reconciliation is theirs to initiate.

In the classic work of Jewish wisdom, *Ethics of the Fathers*, the sages taught, "In a place where there are no human beings, be a human being." In other words, do the right thing regardless of what another person does. Here are some ways to develop the strength to do so:

1. Imagine someone you admire. Ask yourself what he or she would do if he or she were you. Those in the Christian faith ask, "What would Jesus do?" A Jewish version of this question might be, as Rabbi Rami Shapiro once put it, "What Would a Mensch Do?" Think about what the answer would be, and follow it.

2. Begin the process. Trust that the rest will take care of itself. In Jewish tradition, the sages tell a story of a king who had a son who left him because of something the king had done. The king missed the son greatly and tried to find him to reconcile. He did not know where he was, but he went out in search. The son also wanted to reconcile, but he did not know his way back to the castle. He went out in search. They met in the middle.

Forgiveness often works that way. Once we begin, forces are set in motion that help us find understanding and reconciliation.

3. Look for the best in the other person. Even if we were wronged, we can still try to see the other as a human being. They must have some good qualities. Look for them, and think of them as you gain the impetus to forgive.

How Would I Feel If the Relationship Was Repaired?

We may have learned to live with a broken relationship. Life goes on. We can't hold ourselves prisoner to another person's actions. Life demands a certain kind of healing.

In the Bible, Jacob and Esau have this kind of "non-relationship" for 20 years. Each seems to forget about the other, marrying, having children and going on with their lives. Yet, they are twins. They are brothers. When Jacob returns to his homeland, Esau awaits him.

Initially, Jacob is terrified. He is not sure what to expect, but feels that violence from Esau is likely. He even divides his family into groups so that at least part of them will survive if Esau attacks. Yet, when they finally meet, they embrace. They catch up. They reconcile. They move on with their lives.

Did it need to take 20 years? Probably not. The key is to not remain silent. Just as a scab conceals a hidden wound, silence can hide a hurting heart. Envisioning a healing reconciliation can strengthen our motivation. How can we find there?

1. Picture the way forgiveness would feel. Neuroscientists and psychologists have long known about the power of imagery. When we picture – in as much detail as

possible – how forgiveness would feel, we subconsciously take steps and make changes in our mindset to help make it happen.

2. Talk to your pastor or rabbi. Forgiveness is a core part of the Judeo-Christian tradition. A trusted religious leader can offer you a different perspective that can increase motivation for forgiving.

3. Remember that forgiveness does not mean becoming best friends. Jacob and Esau reconcile. They embrace. They talk. Then they go their separate ways. They no longer harbor animosity toward each other, yet they do not spend all their time together. Forgiveness gives you permission to move on and live with greater peace.

If Not Now, When?

Jewish legend tells a story of a man in prison. The king in the area proclaims that he will allow the prisoners one day of freedom. They can each choose they day they want to be free. The Jewish prisoner thinks he should choose Passover, which celebrates the freedom of the Israelites from Egypt. Or perhaps he should choose Yom Kippur, the holiest day of the Jewish year, and he could join his family in the synagogue.

He decides to ask his rabbi the next time the rabbi visits the prison. When he does so, the rabbi tells him the choice is easy. "Do it right now," he says. "Today. You don't know if another day will ever come. Choose freedom for today."

The same sentiment can shape our approach to forgiveness. It is easy to ignore the important for the sake of the urgent. It is easy to put off what we know is important, but which is not a life-or-death emergency today. Forgiveness often falls in that category. We know we should pursue it, but we find it tempting and easy to put it off.

Don't let yourself do it. Contemporary theologian Frederic Buechner echoed the message of Jewish legend when he proclaimed that today is the only day there is: "The point is to see today for what it is because it will be gone before you know it. If you waste it, it is your life that you are wasting. If you look the other way, it may be the moment you've been waiting for always that you're missing. All other days have either disappeared into darkness and oblivion or not yet emerged from them. Today is the only day there is."

SECTION II: IDEAS

Chapter 5: How To Discover Your Life's Purpose

"Life isn't about finding yourself. Life is about creating yourself."
George Bernard Shaw

Why Purpose Matters: A Story

One of the best-selling children's books of all time – and one that I happen to have memorized – is *Goodnight Moon*. It tells of a little boy's bedtime routine. He lies down. He looks around his room. And then he says goodnight to everything he sees.

> Goodnight Moon
> Goodnight room
> Good night cow jumping over the moon
> Goodnight light
> And the red balloon
> Goodnight bears
> Goodnight chairs
> Goodnight kittens
> And goodnight mittens
> Goodnight clocks
> And goodnight socks
> Goodnight little house
> And goodnight mouse
> Goodnight stars
> Goodnight air
> Goodnight noises everywhere

That's it. All is calm in the world. He goes to sleep. What makes this simple story so powerful? Part of it is the rhythm. The words unfold with a familiar and comforting tempo. Another part is the sense of completion. The boy names every object he sees. When he's done, his world is complete. He is at peace. He's ready to sleep.

There are, however, deeper explanations of the book's power. Going to sleep – whether we are children or adults – is hard. We feel anxiety, unresolved issues, fears of the future, concerns for our children and friends. We yearn for the ability to name and resolve our concerns as the little boy does. We yearn for that comfort and sense that all is right in the world.

Yet, we know life is not that simple. We cannot name and understand every object we see. We can become confused, scared, frustrated. As we grow older, we learn that the world is infinitely vast and complex.

We can approach this complexity in a number of ways. We can seek to return to the simplicity of the little boy's room. We can try to make our world small and airtight – to live only with the familiar and comfortable.

But Jewish tradition gives us a different path. It asks us not to despair amidst the challenges and complexities of life. Rather, it encourages us to constantly ask ourselves if we are living at our best. Are we fulfilling our purpose?

What Are We Here On Earth To Do?

I first asked myself this question on a trip to Israel. When I was 16, my grandfather took my cousins and me there. It was a ten-day trip for grandparents and grandchildren. My grandfather, who was 82 at the time, was the oldest person on the trip. He walked slowly and with some pain. My grandmother was in the early stages of Alzheimer's disease. Yet, he insisted on taking us. He pushed himself to go. Throughout the trip, he would usually stay on the bus while we

climbed Masada or visited the Galilee. But we'd talk each
night after dinner. He'd tell us how excited he was to be there
with us.

During this trip, as I was developing a love of Israel, I was
discovering something about my family and about being
Jewish. They were connected. I saw my life and my choices as
connected to what my grandfather and my people had done. A
new path, a new possibility, opened before me. The path did
not unfold rapidly or directly. A choice my grandfather made
transformed my future. It led to what my pastor friends
describe as "a calling" – a desire to serve and devote our lives
to something larger than ourselves. *It is not just rabbis or
priests or ministers who have callings – each of us do.*

What Is Your Calling?

Figuring out our calling can be overwhelming. What is harder
than understanding ourselves? What is more challenging than
determining what unique gifts we bring to a world of over six
billion people? But I am absolutely convinced that it is not
impossible. We start with examining our actions.

What motivates what we do? What in our heart helps us get up
each morning? An initial answer might be our family. We work
hard to support those we love. We center our lives around our
children or our elderly parents. We wake up early, endure the
traffic, sit at our computers late at night, so that we can create a
prosperous and happy life for our family. We fret when our
children and grandchildren face difficulties and celebrate in
their successes and character.

While family is essential, when it comes to questions of
purpose, it is not an end in itself. Caring for our family is, I
think, like breathing. It is a core part of life. Yet, we do not

exist simply to breathe. Similarly, our children do not come into this world just to provide us with a purpose for living. As parents, we care for, nurture and support our children. We help them develop their talents and find their calling and purpose, just as we uncover our own.

What Victor Frankl Discovered During The Holocaust

The way we uncover our own is captured by the Holocaust survivor and psychiatrist Victor Frankl. Frankl wrote the classic text *Man's Search for Meaning*. The meaning of life, he argued, is not some secret that we uncover by reading the right book or meeting the right guru. No, it is *something that is unique to each of us, and it is something that is not so much discovered as created.* We create the meaning of our lives through the actions – large and small – that we take. At the same time, it is not just random actions that we accumulate and then decide will constitute our purpose. It is the actions we take as part of a conscious decision to devote our lives to something larger, more significant, more enduring than ourselves.

In fact, Frankl said three things can shape that decision. "We discover meaning in life," he writes, "by doing a deed, by experiencing a value and by suffering." These three are not indivisible. In fact, they often coincide.

They coincided in a wonderful rabbi and leader I once met named Alfred Gottschalk, who passed away right after I was ordained as a rabbi. When we met, Dr. Gottschalk told the story of how he grew up in Oberwessel, a small German town. He was eight years old when Nazi storm troopers burst into his school room and shouted for the Jewish students to leave. Soon thereafter came *Kristallnacht,* the night of broken glass. Synagogues were destroyed and Torah scrolls burned. The next morning, Dr. Gottschalk's grandfather took him to the stream behind their desecrated synagogue to retrieve the torn fragments of the congregation's Torah scroll. "Alfred," his grandfather said, "someday, you will put the pieces back together." In that moment, an eight-year-old boy found his purpose. He transformed an experience of suffering to a life of deeds grounded in the values of the Jewish people.

In contrast to Dr. Frankl, however, Jewish wisdom does not suggest that we have to suffer in order to find meaning. Rather, we can look at ourselves and our choices by answering three questions. These questions, I believe, are familiar to all of us.

Three Questions To Ask Yourself

1. "If I am not for myself," Rabbi Hillel asked 2000 years ago, "who will be for me?" In other words, if what I do does not come from my heart, why am I doing it?

When what we do doesn't reflect our ideals and commitments, it doesn't meet our purpose. Indeed, we can be very good and successful at something, yet still find it lacks meaning. Even further, we may not be doing it as well as we could. Professor Daniel Pink published a book several years ago entitled *Drive*. It is about what truly motivates high-performing people. What he found was that money and stature are not nearly as important as the deeply felt human need to direct our own lives, to learn and create new things, and to do better by ourselves and our world. How powerful and true!

Sometimes it's hard to meet these criteria. We're not always going to feel in control and creative and great about what we are doing. Every job and important thing in life – like parenting – has its difficulties and drudgery. There are practical ways we can figure out what brings out our best. If, for example, I go a few days or a week without writing, I know it. My spirit feels drained and my mind wanders. But all I have to do is start again, and the passion returns. Each of us has similar passions we can follow. When our work touches our deepest selves, the routine, as Abraham Joshua Heschel put it, can become the amazing.

2. "If I am only for myself, what am I?" We do not connect with God only through individual experiences. Satisfaction does not arrive simply when we do only what makes us feel good. It comes when we serve others. As theologian Frederic Buechner put it, "The kind of work God usually calls us to do is the kind of work (a) that we need most to do and (b) that the world most needs to have done... The place God calls us to is the place where our deep gladness and the world's deep hunger meet."

Consider that phrase – "the world's deep hunger." Each of us brings a dish to help meet that deep hunger. When we help meet that hunger, we also meet our own. Nothing nourishes us like giving of ourselves.

As a rabbi, I learn this every day through the families of community members who have passed away. *When I ask family members about the deceased's life, rather than talk about work or money, they talk about family and character. Indeed, I have noticed that the ones who are most missed are not necessarily the most successful and famous.*

They are the ones who enhanced the lives of others. They are the ones who, like my grandfather, constantly did small acts that helped their communities and the people they loved. And invariably, family members tell me that the deceased gained more from their kindness than they gave. In lifting up others, they found themselves uplifted. "If I am only for myself, what am I?"

3. "And if not now, when?" One of the best ways to uncover our purpose is to start doing something now. Pastor Rick Warren of California wrote the best-selling book of the last decade. Entitled *The Purpose-Driven Life*, it is a Christian thinker's perspective on what can bring meaning and focus to life. One of Warren's insights resonates with Hillel's imperatives as well. As Warren writes, "If you want your life to have impact, focus it! Stop dabbling. Stop trying to do it all. Do less. Prune away even good activities and do only that which matters most. Never confuse activity with productivity. You can be busy without a purpose, but what's the point?"

He's right. Discovering our purpose gives a point to our lives. A story is told of Rabbi Hayim of Volozhin, the leader of a famed nineteenth century school. As a boy he was an indifferent student. One day he decided to abandon his studies and enter a trade school. He announced the decision to his parents, who reluctantly acquiesced. That night the young man had a dream. In it an angel held a stack of beautiful books. "Whose books are those?" he asked. "They are yours," the angel replied, "if you have the courage to write them." That night changed the young man's life. Hayim was on the way to discovering who he was meant to become.

The future does not exist. It is created by what we do. It is shaped by the choices we make. Will today be the beginning of a renewed self? Will we shape our future so that it reflects our deepest hopes and beliefs? When we discover our purpose, we discover what God put us on this earth to do.

Chapter 6: How To Deal With Anger

"For every minute you remain angry, you give up sixty seconds of peace of mind." Ralph Waldo Emerson

Several years ago, I was a camp counselor discussing some camper problems with the director, and he said something I have never forgotten: "There is no right or wrong; only consequences." Now I don't agree with this statement wholeheartedly. Certain things are right or wrong, even if they are done in secret and therefore do not have foreseeable consequences. But his statement does apply, I think, to emotions or feelings we have. Certain feelings are not right or wrong. The way we evaluate them depends on their consequences.

Take fear, for example. Sometimes fear is harmful – for example if someone afraid to leave their home or drive their car. But sometimes fear is helpful. If you are afraid that your friend has had too much to drink and you do not want to get in a car with him, your fear has helped you. Or if you are afraid you will get caught cheating and therefore you don't, I'd say that's a good thing. The same is true of anger. Anger, at times, can be a helpful emotion. It was African Americans angry with the way they had been treated who inspired and led the civil rights movement. The Biblical Prophets – Amos, Isaiah, Jeremiah – were angry at the way the poor, the widow and the orphan were treated. Their anger was constructive.

However, perhaps more often than not, anger is destructive. Each of us has probably been in a situation where someone we know lost his or her temper and exploded over some small thing. The consequences were probably (a) we looked at them a bit differently, surprised at the depth of his or her anger, and (b) their rage was not helpful in getting what they desired. The first century Roman historian and philosopher Plutarch pointed this out in an essay he wrote entitled *On the Control of Anger*: "We who tame wild beasts and make them gentle…under the impulse of rage cast off children, friends and companions, let loose our wrath, like some wild beast, on servants and fellow citizens."

What Happens When Biblical Heroes Get Angry

The Bible tells an interesting story of anger. It centers around a conflict between an important Israelite leader named Korach and Moses. Korach sees Moses as a dictator, exerting unjust authority over the people. Along with several supporters, he challenges Moses: He says to him, "You have gone too far!... Why do you raise yourself above God's people?" Moses pleas with Korach's supporters, telling them that he does not seek power for himself. He is simply doing God's will. This only intensifies their rage. "Is it not enough," they ask, "that you brought us from a land flowing with milk and honey to have us die in the wilderness, that you would also lord it over us? Even if you had brought us to a land flowing with milk and honey, and given us possession of fields and vineyards, should you gouge out those men's eyes?" Moses then tells Korach, his family and his followers to gather at the tent of meeting. *They are instantly swallowed into the earth.* The next day, when Korach's followers express their anger to Moses, a plague strikes the people, killing 14,000 more of them.

If we step back and look at what happened, we see the consequences of uncontrolled anger. In his rage and confrontation, Korach sparked only death and destruction. And Moses himself had little patience for negotiation. Of course, the text indicates that Moses was simply doing God's bidding. Yet, we know that Moses had a fiery temper. He shattered the tablets of the Ten Commandments when he saw the golden calf. In another instance, he struck a rock to produce water, rather than speak to it, as God had instructed. This was a problem because it indicated to the people that Moses had divine powers, whereas he was simply God's instrument and should have made that clear. The sages tell us that it was on account of his impulsive temper that Moses was not permitted to enter the Promised Land. With Korach and with Moses, their anger becomes self-destructive.

I don't think we can really prevent feelings of anger. Except perhaps in extraordinary people like Gandhi, anger is natural. It is likely a consequence of evolution, serving as a survival mechanism that helped our ancestors defend themselves. The relevant question for us is what can we do to control our anger? How do we prevent it from becoming destructive and hurtful and channel it into productive work?

How To Use Anger Wisely

Jewish wisdom can be quite instructive. In one of the sayings in the classic book of Jewish wisdom, *Ethics of the Fathers*, Rabbi Eliezer says: "Let your friend's honor be as dear to you as your own, do not be easily angered, and repent one day before you die." These statements are interconnected. If your friend's honor is dear to you, you will respect him by not insulting or exploding at him in rage. In other words, respect for others is a way of checking anger. And the last statement, "repent one day before you die," is a call for putting things in perspective. If each of us is aware that we might die tomorrow, we won't explode over petty things. Thus, respecting others and looking at our lives from a broad perspective help us control feelings of anger.

A second suggestion is to prevent legitimate anger from becoming personal. As Rabbi Joseph Telushkin puts it, "No matter how upset you are, restrict the expression of your anger to the incident that provoked it… As long as we keep our words focused on the one incident, we are unlikely to say anything that will destroy a relationship." What Telushkin is getting at, I think, is our tendency to take our anger out on others. In fact, we often direct our anger at the wrong source. If we've had a hard day at work, we might take it out on our spouse. If we're having problems at home, we might take it out on our staff.

Or let's take a more prosaic example. We make a reservation at a restaurant. When we arrive, we have to wait an hour for a table. We might become quite angry at the host or hostess. When we finally sit down, we may even take it out on the waitress. But each of us probably knows that it's likely neither person's fault. We have expressed our anger at the restaurant's inefficient system on a person whose job it is to seat us or to serve our meals. Directing anger at its proper source can prevent it from becoming destructive.

Another important way to avoid impulsive anger is finding a mild and wise confidante. Once again, Pirke Avot instructs each of us "to find for ourselves a teacher; and make for a ourselves a friend." If we get angry at something someone said to us, such a friend might say, "Oh, so and so said that to you. Perhaps he didn't mean it in the way you think." The least helpful friend – one we should avoid in these instances – is the person who makes matters worse, the person who says, "He said that? I can't believe it. What are you going to do about it?" To check our impulsive impulses, we need the former, not the latter.

Don't Act Too Quickly--Sleep On It

A final piece of Jewish wisdom paraphrases a well-known

saying: Before responding to something or someone that makes us angry, we should sleep on it. If at all possible, we should give ourselves time to reflect before saying something rash or harmful. A rabbinic sage writes that whenever he became enraged, he would check into the *Shulchan Aruch*, the massive sixteenth century Jewish legal code, to see whether he had the right to be angry in such a circumstance. Not surprisingly, he found that going to his library, taking down the book, and checking it through calmed him down. Each of us can cultivate techniques to calm us down: go for a run or a drive, talk to a friend, watch a movie. The way we then respond to the situation will likely be more thoughtful and productive.

Moses and Korach let anger dissolve into impulsive confrontation. We can learn from their failure. We can strive for the empathy, the self-knowledge, the mentors and the wisdom to transform those feelings of hurtful anger into righteous and thoughtful enthusiasm.

Chapter 7: A Covenant of the Spirit

"Man is always in God's presence, and God should always be present to man." Martin Buber

Judaism has a long history of debate. In fact, there is a classic Jewish joke: When you have two Jews in a room together, you have at least three opinions. Debate and discussion is seen as an act of the Jewish sages called *l'shem shamyaim* – for the service of heaven. Debate helps us discern what God desires us to do.

Two thousand years ago, one interesting debate focused on the lighting of the Hanukkah candles. Hanukkah is the Jewish holiday that often occurs around the same time as Christmas. For eight consecutive nights, we light candles, beginning with one and concluding with eight, with one head candle, called the *shamash* in the middle. Typically, the *shamash* is used to light each of the other candles. What happens, however, if the candles are lit, and one burns out? Must we use the *shamash* once again to light that candle? Or are we permitted to use one of the other regular candles to rekindle the one that burned out?

This seems like a very minor question. Yet, a profound truth is found in both the debate and the answer. One rabbi says we can only use the *shamash*. He reasons that when we use one regular candle to light another candle, we diminish the light, strength and holiness of the first candle. Another rabbi says it is permissible. When we use one candle to light another, we do not diminish light. We do not detract from it. Rather, *we increase it. Both lights can burn brightly, and more light is brought into the world.* This view became the law.

How Sharing Your Faith Strengthens It

The same principle applies, I believe, to religion. When we share our light with one another the flame of faith burns brighter. Neither faith is diminished. Rather, they are both enriched. When we share our beliefs and traditions with one another, as this book strives to do, we deepen our own faith while growing in appreciation and gratitude for the God of us all.

A unifying theme for many faiths is covenant. The Hebrew word for covenant is *brit*. It connotes a sacred relationship, a commitment between God and the Jewish people. It began with Abraham. It was affirmed by Moses in the Exodus from Egypt. And it was sealed with the entire people through the giving and acceptance of the Torah, the five books of Moses, at Mount Sinai.

Yet, that is only the beginning. The rabbinic interpreters refer to this *brit* as a *brit olam* – an eternal covenant. It is dynamic. It is not frozen in one time and place. It is rooted in the past, yet evolves into the future. We are meant to hear the word of God in the present tense. We are meant to listen for its message for our time. Martin Buber put it such: "The eternal revelation is here and now. I do not believe in a self-definition of God prior to the experience of human beings.... The eternal voice of strength flows, the eternal voice sounds forth to us now."

How To Live *With* The Past, Not *In* The Past

Buber's conception may sound mystical, but it also eminently practical and relevant for us today. Rabbi Jonathan Sacks paints a picture of what it means in action in a beautiful story about an encounter he had. Rabbi Sacks was the Chief Rabbi of Great Britain from 1990-2013, and his work included investigating several cutting-edge questions of medical ethics. In this capacity, he met with Lord Robert Winston, one of the world's leading researchers on In Vitro Fertilization, embryo development and the human genome.

During their visit in Lord Winston's office, Sacks noticed a copy of the Five Books of Moses, wedged between volumes of the latest scientist research. In addition, several volumes of commentary, along with a prayer book, sat near them. Even though he is a cutting-edge scientist pushing the boundaries of life, Lord Winston is a deeply religious man whose faith guides him in the critical work he does. For him the covenant is ongoing, continuing to guide his work and values.

As people of faith, Christians and Jews, this notion of ongoing covenant matters deeply. *We do not live in the past. Rather, we live with the past, drawing from the accumulated wisdom of our tradition in order to build a better future.* We see our lives part of a journey that began before us, continues after us, and is carried forward by and through us. That is what it means to be part of a covenant.

We Are People Of The Spirit

Our challenge is to shape the meaning of that covenant, to make sure that it is not defined only by the past, solely by what was. The past – the way things used to be – can become an idol. We can worship it amidst the confusion, speed and significance of the challenges we face. When we become fearful and confused, when we seek easy answers to complex questions, *literalism can replace logic. Obedience can replace openness. Arrogance can replace engagement. Stubbornness can replace spirit.*

Recently I came across a story about a great Protestant

theologian, Paul Tillich. After he delivered a lecture, a passionate young man ran up to him. "Mr. Tillich," he said, "do you or do you not believe that every single syllable of scripture is the inspired word of God?" Tillich replied, "If the spirit is greater than the letter, yes. If the letter is greater than the spirit, no!"

We are people of the spirit. The future of a meaningful and living faith depends on us. I believe this spirit of openness – this ability to change and grow as part of an eternal covenant – is one of the lessons of the Israelite experience in Egypt.

Consider that seminal scene in the Book of Exodus where Moses negotiates with Pharaoh. He begs Pharaoh to "Let my people go." Pharaoh has so far refused. Yet, at one point, we seem to glimpse a change of heart. During the seventh plague, hail, Pharaoh summons Moses and Aaron and says, "This time I have sinned. The Lord is in the right, and I and my people are in the wrong." But as soon as the plague is over he changes his mind. "He and his officials," the text tells us, "hardened their hearts" (Exodus 9:34).

Moses and Aaron respond by telling Pharaoh of the next plague, locusts. This forecast seems to change the minds of Pharaoh's officials. They are ready to relent. They see that Egypt has been devastated by the plagues, and they need to change course. They say to Pharaoh in exasperation, "How long will this man be a snare to us? Let the people go, so that they may worship the Lord their God. Do you not yet realize that Egypt is ruined?"

Pharaoh, however, will have none of it. He will not change course. He will not relent. He will fight Moses and Aaron to the bitter end. What was wrong with Pharaoh? Couldn't he see what was right in front of him? Was he simply that foolish?

Was his hate so great that it blinded him to reality?

The March Of Folly

These are all plausible explanations. Perhaps, however, Pharaoh's story is more complicated than that. In 1984, historian Barbara Tuchman wrote a book entitled *The March of Folly*. It looked at a challenging historical phenomenon: Throughout history, intelligent leaders and people have made decisions that led to their and their people's destruction. Tuchman was not trying to understand decisions that, in retrospect, turned out to be wrong ones. We all have those. Uncertainty is a part of life; sometimes we get it right, and other times we get it wrong. Tuchman, rather, was exploring a different question. The question of why some people make decisions that are unequivocally contrary to their own interests. Her examples range from the Trojan's decision to admit the Greek horse into their city, to the British Empire's loss of the American colonies. In each of these instances, unambiguous warnings of impending disasters were ignored and rejected. Obstinacy replaced reason.

Perhaps the same phenomenon happened with Pharaoh. He clung to a world he knew even as it fell apart in front of him. It was a world where he was seen as a god and absolute ruler. In that context, through the lenses through which he saw the world, relenting to Israelite demands was unthinkable. If he let the Israelites go, he would be showing signs of weakness and capitulation. His power would be undermined. His infallibility would be diminished. His people might rebel. His world would be broken.

Pharaoh's pride – his folly – allows the Israelites to escape. When they arrive at Mount Sinai, they enter into a new kind of covenant. It is a *brit olam*, an eternal covenant, rooted not in might nor power. But rather, as the prophet Zechariah put it, in *ruach* – spirit. It is this spirit that allows us, Jews and Christians, to see the beliefs and texts of our traditions in a new light, speaking to us clearly in our time and in our lives. It is this spirit that must guide us as we work together, learning from one another, in the task of *tikkun olam* (repair of our world), *b'malchut shaddai* (with strength and support from the God of us all).

Each of us is part of a covenant. A covenant with God, a covenant with our religious community, a covenant with our families, a covenant with our past and future. We hold up that covenant with our hearts. We hold it up with our hands. And we hold it up, together, with our spirits.

SECTION III: GOD

Chapter 8: How To Hear God's Alarm Clock

"The most important challenge is not learning how to live after death, it's learning how to live after birth." Steven Carr Reuben

What distinguishes the Jewish holiday of *Rosh Hashanah* (Head of the Year) from every other holiday is the sounding of the shofar (a ram's horn). Indeed, one of the other names for Rosh Hashanah is *Yom Teruah*, the day of the sounding of the shofar. To hear the sound of the shofar is the primary purpose of the day.

What's so important about the shofar? Why must we hear it? The most insightful answer I've heard was given by Rabbi Harold Kushner. While the words of this prayer book are addressed to God, he noted, *the sounds of the Shofar are addressed to us.* "It's a wakeup call, an alarm clock; as if God were saying to us, 'Don't just plead with me for a year of life. I'm giving you life; what are you doing with it?'"

In other words, the shofar is an alarm clock for our lives. It pierces through our routines and habits. It awakens us from the slumber of everyday living. It challenges us to think, to question, to wake up! What are we doing with the challenges and opportunities life puts before us? What meanings are we making out of the experiences we face?

Remember The Important Questions

The shofar does not just present these questions; it also gives us a framework for discovering their answers. Each of the three traditional blasts – *tekiah* (an unbroken blast lasting about three seconds), *shevarim* (a *tekiah* broken into three segments), and *terua*h (three rapid-fire, short blasts) – offer us criteria by which we can look at our lives. They capture the range of our longings, emotions and needs.

The first sound, *tekiah*, summons us to human connection and community. The Torah itself tells us that the original function of the *tekiah* sound was to assemble the people. Summer camps often have a bell that rings when it's time to gather for a meal or ceremony. The *tekiah* sound does the same thing: it commands us to gather, coming together so that we can live more fully.

We need that reminder. In a society that makes it easy to be alone – to entertain ourselves on the computer or with our iPhones – we can forget the richness that comes in living with and for others. Life gains meaning when we share it. Martin Buber, the great theologian of the twentieth century, made this message his life's work. When Buber was asked where God was found, he did not say in heaven. He did not even say God is everywhere. He said "God lives in relationships."

Buber taught this lesson with his books and his own life. In his autobiography he told a story about a time when a student came to him with a problem. Buber was a young university professor in the midst of his studies when this young student knocked on his office door. He looked quite troubled. He asked Buber if he could speak with him for a few minutes. Buber agreed, but with a clear signal of impatience. He nodded as the student talked, though his mind was on other things. When the student finished speaking, Buber shared some thoughts and reflections, and then got up and wished the student well. That night Buber noted in his diaries that he had not been fully present with the student. He had not discerned his true question and probed what lay behind his troubles. He subsequently learned that the student had taken his own life.

Human relationships are like water. They quench the thirst for connection that make life meaningful. The rabbinic sages put it more bluntly—*"achevruta o mituta*, friendship or death."

The sound of Shofar reminds us to be grateful for the gift of one another. To marvel at the love of our family and friends, children and grandchildren, those upon whom we depend and those who depend upon us. *Tekiah* proclaims the blessings we give to one another.

Brokenness Is A Part Of Life

The second sound we hear is *shevarim*. The word *shevarim* comes from the Hebrew root *shevar*, which means broken. *Shevarim* is the plaintive sound of brokenness. It acknowledges the sadness we all face. The broken dreams, broken relationships, broken hearts. Why do we need to hear this sound on Rosh Hashanah? Rosh Hashanah is a day of happiness. It is a day we eat apples and honey. It begins the New Year.

The Torah wisely understands, however, that brokenness is a part of life. In fact, we live more fully when we acknowledge and confront the imperfections, challenges, and disappointments we all face. We may not always be able to fix what is broken. But we can respond in a way that enhances and gives greater depth and meaning to our lives. We treat life as more precious when we realize how fragile it is.

How A Wedding Taught Me The Meaning Of Life

A wedding ceremony I performed a few years ago drove home this truth for me. The bride was a friend of a friend. She called to tell me that she was engaged. They had a wedding date set for the following June. Would I be available? Sure, I replied.

"But, there's more," she said softly. "My mom is dying. She has pancreatic cancer. She insists we not change our plans for the big ceremony in June." She asked if I could come to her hospital room and perform a wedding ceremony so her mom would have a chance to see them married.

"Of course," I said. We set a date. When the time came, I went over to Northwestern Hospital. I wore my usual office attire: a striped, button-down shirt, grey pants, loafers. When I got to the hospital room, I quickly realized I had made a significant fashion mishap. The bride stood outside the room in her wedding gown. The groom beamed next to her in a tuxedo. At least 25 friends in suits, ties, dresses, and make up, crowded the hospital room. They stood around the mom's bed. A hospital worker had brought in an electric keyboard and began playing. Four men brought in a portable canopy covered in flowers. The bride and groom entered to music and song.

Overwhelmed with emotion, I had trouble beginning the ceremony. We succeeded, however, in getting through it. By the end, there was not a dry eye in the room. When the groom broke the glass, the applause bristled with a mixture of joy and sadness, hope and pain. We knew life had just given us a rare moment of beauty amidst tragedy. About three weeks later the bride's mom passed away.

The bride did not have to do what she did. She could have remained angry at life, distancing herself from feelings of love and commitment because of what happened to the person she loved most dearly. Many people do respond to tragedy in such way. They conclude, as Shakespeare put it, that life is "a tale told by an idiot, full of sound and fury, signifying nothing." Why should we take life seriously when the more seriously we take it, the more likely it is to break out hearts?

Jewish tradition, however, offers us the opposite view. We take life seriously because it is uncertain. Life's uncertainties make it all the more precious and valuable. When a crack appears in the vessel of our lives, we need not let it shatter the whole thing. Rather, as the singer-songwriter Leonard Cohen put it, the cracks are where we let the light in.

How To See God In A Broken World

The final shofar sound is *teruah*. The *teruah* sound intends to proclaim God's sovereignty over the universe. It resembles the blast of trumpets that would traditionally precede the entry of a king or queen. On Rosh Hashanah, we sound the shofar to usher in God's presence for the New Year. We acknowledge God's majesty here on earth.

We may find it very difficult to do so. How can we say that God governs the universe when bad things happen so often to good people? How can we say it when disease, suffering, poverty and tragic death afflict so many? We ask these questions. At the same time, we yearn to believe. We yearn to believe that some power, some force in the universe makes for justice, beauty, life.

The sound of *teruah* tells us to look for that power. To do so, we look behind the surface. We read beyond the headlines. One of those headlines this past summer told of a series of murders in Norway. A lone gunman burst into a government building and killed eight people. He then made his way to an island where a political party was holding its youth retreat. He landed on the island and began shooting. People jumped into the water. Sixty-nine people were killed.

In the midst of this tragedy, however, a small miracle took place. I learned of it in a story buried on the Google News website. It told of a couple – two females – who were having a picnic on the other side of the lake from the island. They saw smoke coming up from it. They heard gunfire and screaming. Sensing something awful was happening, they hopped in their motorboat. Then they saw young people jumping into the water in order to escape the gunfire on the island. They drove the boat to the people they saw, pulled them in, and drove them to safety. As the right side of their boat became riddled with gunshots, they made four return trips, saving an estimated 40 young adults from drowning or death.

Such an act of courage does not negate the horror of what transpired. Yet, *it is in these acts of courage that God's presence becomes real. In them we catch a glimpse of a world filled with hope, goodness and love.*

The Enduring Lesson Of Anne Frank

One of the greatest champions of this vision was a girl named Anne Frank. We probably know her story. Hidden from the Nazis with her parents in Amsterdam, she kept a diary. She wrote in the diary for more than two years. In August 1944 she and her family were found. She perished in a concentration camp. Her diary, however, made it out. It became one of the most important books of the twentieth century. To me the most powerful comment in the diary is perhaps its most famous. "It's really a wonder," she wrote, "that I haven't dropped all my ideals, because they seem so absurd and impossible to carry out. Yet I keep them, because in spite of everything I still believe that people are really good at heart." Just imagine the contrast here: The Nazi army is sweeping across Europe. Villages destroyed, millions of people killed. Yet, in a tiny attic in a hidden apartment was a girl celebrating human goodness. With light from a tiny crack, she was writing in a diary that would inspire millions and change the world.

I recently learned something new about the creation of this diary. A group of preservationists was working to restore the attic where Anne Frank wrote into its original condition. In doing so, they found a single photograph she kept on the wall. It was a photo of a Norwegian ice skater and actress from the 1930s named Sonja Haney. In the photo, the spotlight shines down on Haney, who poses on the ice in magnificent form.

The preservation of that image, and of Anne Frank's diary, tells us something. It tells us that what remains, what persists, what moves us even amidst terror, is the beauty and the sanctity of the human spirit. As we hear the sound of the shofar, we recognize that beauty. We hear its plaintive cry. And we let it carry and guide our hearts, hands and spirits.

Chapter 9: Our Struggles With God Make Us Better Human Beings

"The human story simply cannot be told without reference to that mystery and majesty that transcends all logic and reason. Only those who open themselves to such a mystery can confront the complexities of their lives, the brightness and the darkness, without being blinded by life's grandeur or crushed by its terror." Alexander Schindler

A friend and fellow parent told me the following story. When her youngest daughter was six or seven, she and her husband used to read to her before bed. A little conversation would follow. Then, before they turned off the lights, the daughter would ask them, "Do you believe in God?" Dad would say, "Yes, absolutely." Mom would say a bit more, talking about her various feelings and questions.

This routine continued for several weeks. Finally, one evening the daughter asked the same question, "Do you believe in God?" Dad said yes, mom started her winding and thoughtful explanation. After a few minutes, her frustration growing, the little girl finally shouted: "Would you just say you believe in God?!"

What Do We Want From God?

This young girl desired a simple answer. This desire reflects a yearning for order and stability in this confusing world. Especially at a young age, we want to know that everything is okay and that the world makes sense.

Sigmund Freud linked this yearning to the helpless infant's dependence on mother and father. Like a baby relies on his parents, each of us, throughout life, yearns for a powerful and authoritative figure who can help us make sense of life. We call this figure God. Some people maintain the parental image of God throughout their lives. Others develop a different – what we might call a more mature view of God – seeing God not as all-powerful, but as some kind of force for goodness and order in the universe. Many of the theologians of liberal Christianity and Judaism fall within this camp. Still others, however, are simply perplexed. They don't know what to believe about God.

I see this trend within the Jewish community and statistical studies seem to bear it out. According to recent study, about half of the 5.3 million Jews in America identify themselves as "secular" or "somewhat secular." Whereas 95 percent of Americans profess belief in God or some kind of higher power, another recent survey indicated that about 60 to 70 percent of Jews claim such a belief (2003 Harris Interactive Poll).

What can we make of this? Does belief in God matter to Jews? Must it be something we embrace? My answer is *Yes, but.* God is central to who we are. Our Jewish approach to God has shaped Western civilization. Yet, Judaism does not ask us to believe in God in the way that the concept of belief is commonly understood.

What Do Jews Believe About God?

First, in Judaism, to believe in God is not to know everything about God. Indeed, the twelfth century Rabbi Joseph Albo said, "If I knew God, I would be God." To believe in God is not say *God does this, this and this.* To believe in God is not say if I do "x," I will go to heaven, or if I do "y," I will be punished. That is not faith. That is hubris.

Rather, the Hebrew word for belief – *emunah* – really means faithfulness. *In Judaism, to believe in God is to be faithful to what God asks and demands of us.* The Bible is our guide to discovering what these demands are. They include the Ten Commandments. Yet, they are much broader than that. They emerge out of an idea about the nature of the universe. The underlying assumption of the Bible and of Judaism is that *there is a moral purpose and order to the universe.* We believe in God if we live our lives with faith in this proposition. We believe in God if we live as if there is more to life than the satisfaction of our own needs and desires, that there is something beyond ourselves that shapes how we live.

One of the greatest Jewish thinkers of the twentieth century, Mordecai Kaplan, put it well when he said, "It matters very little how we conceive God, as long as we so believe in God that belief in Him makes a tremendous difference in our lives." In other words, actions demonstrate belief. Our deeds, rather than our words or logic, illustrate our faith.

A profound example of this type comes, interestingly, from a well-known Catholic figure, Mother Teresa. A few years ago a book of her letters was published. In it she revealed her profound doubts about God's role in her life. She described her feelings of emptiness at prayer and unfulfilled yearning to understand God's truth. Despite her doubts, many in the world continue to see her as an exemplar of faith. She lived her life in a way that responded to God's demands even if she didn't know exactly who or what God is.

God Wants Us To Be Real

In a way, Mother Teresa's doubts humanized her and illustrated the way that genuine faith is within everyone's reach. Rabbi Irwin Kula, reflecting on Mother Teresa's legacy, put it well when he said, "Mother Teresa's honesty about her spiritual emptiness is uncomfortable for us because we tend to see genuine faith and love as free of doubt. But nothing could be further from the truth. *A mature faith and a rich love, a genuine relationship with God or with another person is born of the grit and insecurity of life."* Belief or faith is not certainty. It is the courage to do what is right in a world of uncertainty.

Since Judaism sees belief expressed through action, it follows that the best way to understand God is not as a noun. Rather, God is a verb. God comes into being only as we act in Godly ways. This idea was first proposed by Rabbi Harold Schulweis, who called it predicate theology. According to Schulweis, the important question is not whether we believe that God is caring or that God is merciful, but whether we act in Godly ways by caring for and having mercy on others.

This view fits well with the structure of the Ten Commandments. One of its peculiar features is that the first commandment is not really a commandment. If we read it closely we see that the first commandment is "I am the Lord your God, who brought who out of Egypt, out of the house of bondage." That's it. It's not a commandment. It's a statement. Only when we get to the second commandment do we see an actual command: "You shall have no other gods before me." The familiar other commandments – you shall not steal, you shall not murder, etc – follow. Why this peculiar structure? It's not the same in Christianity, which counts "You shall have no other gods before me" as part of the first commandment. Why does Judaism begin the Ten Commandments with a statement – I am the Lord your God? Because the ultimate commandment is to live up to that statement, to demonstrate that proposition, by following the particular commandments that follow.

How God Works In The World

The relationship between the first commandment and the nine

others is like the relationship between the Declaration of Independence and the Constitution. Like the first commandment, the Declaration of Independence sets out a vision of life, liberty and the pursuit of happiness. Like the other nine commandments, the Constitution is our way of realizing it.

To summarize, the statistics that measure belief in God use the wrong measurements. In Judaism, we don't illustrate belief by words. We demonstrate it by action. We don't see God as an old man in the sky with a beard and a lightning bolt.

We see God when we see the pain and needs of another. We touch God as we reach out to help those in need. We demonstrate our belief in God through the details of our lives. Indeed, in my paraphrase and slight emendation of the prophet Micah's biblical charge: *If* we "do justly and love mercy, *then* we will walk humbly with our God."

Chapter 10: How To Make Your Life A Blessing

As we reach the end of our journey through Jewish wisdom, we can glimpse the path ahead with the following story.

Once upon a time, a wise man met with a king. The king challenged the man with a riddle. He said, "In my hands is a small bird. Is it alive or dead?" The wise man paused and looked down.

The wise man thought to himself, "If I say it is alive, he will close his hand and crush it. If I say it is dead, he will open his hand and let it fly away." The wise man turned his head up and said in a soft yet commanding voice, "It's all in your hands."

The same is true for us. Our lives are in our hands. It is not always going to be easy. We face struggle, challenges and difficulties. Yet, like the Biblical Jacob, we can derive blessings from them. We can, to use the beautiful phrase of the late singer Debbie Friedman, "find the courage to make our lives a blessing."

I believe Judaism's gift to the world is teaching us how to do so. To make our lives blessings, we need to do two things: count our blessings and speak our blessings.

Counting our blessings: As a father of two young children, I am truly blessed. However, that's easy to forget at 3:00 AM when one child's loud crying wakes up the other.

One of the ways I remind myself is by following an ancient Jewish custom. In Judaism the first thing we are supposed to do each morning is sit up and say the words, "I am grateful to you,

Oh God, who has restored my soul from sleep and given me the breath of life."

No sighing. No turning our pillows over and burying our heads in them. We recognize the blessing of life. We prime ourselves to live with gratitude. We count our blessings and find happiness in them.

Saying blessings: It is not enough, however, to recognize and count our blessings. We have to say them. Acknowledge them. Speak them. That's why the ancient Jewish sages urged us to say 100 blessings a day!

Something magical happens when we give expression to our feelings. About a month ago, I saw an example of this magic. I was in my office when a member of my congregation came by. He had a burning question.

"I was dining at a restaurant in New York," he began. "A few tables away from me a man stood up and proposed to his girlfriend. She said yes, and everybody in the restaurant cheered. Then the man walked quietly over to a corner, put on a yamacha (a Jewish ritual head covering), and said some type of blessing. His and his fiance's eyes filled with tears. Rabbi, do you have any idea what blessing he said."

I recited a blessing I thought it might be, and he said, "Yes, that's it! Do you have a copy?" "Sure," I said. "Why do you ask?"

"I am planning to propose to my girlfriend this weekend, and I want to say it with her."

With tears in my eyes, I handed him the blessing.

How A Blessing Works

Blessings express our feelings. They need not be traditional ones. They simply need to come from the heart. When they do, they can change our lives.

I experienced this truth near the end of my grandfather's life. We were very close. Up until his death, I tried to talk to or visit him every day. We would usually end our conversations with my saying "Talk to you tomorrow." We did not say, "I love you." He was not a warm fuzzy kind of guy, and it just did not feel right.

But during the last few weeks of his life, something changed. Perhaps it was the birth of my daughter, Hannah, or perhaps it was his declining condition. Our moments became more fused with meaning.

When I Said I Love You

A month before he died, I was sitting by his bed and we were talking. As I got up to leave, I felt a twitch in my stomach. I turned to him and said, "Grandpa, I love you." He didn't say anything.

But our connection had changed. Thereafter, we ended each conversation with my saying "I love you." Saying I love you to our dearest ones blesses them and us. It is a way we make our lives a blessing. It is something each of us can do today, tomorrow and for the rest of our lives.

About The Author

Evan Moffic is the Rabbi of the historic Congregation Solel in suburban Chicago. He writes for the world's largest multi-faith website Beliefnet.Com, and lectures at churches, synagogue and interfaith centers across the United States.

Connect with Me

I would love to hear from you. You can e-mail me at emoffic@solel.org. You may also visit my personal website, which serves as a hub for articles, videos, sermons and public speaking presentations. It is found at **www.rabbimoffic.com.**